FREEDOM FIGHTER

WILLIAM WALLACE AND SCOTLAND'S BATTLE FOR INDEPENDENCE

by Don Nardo

Content Adviser: James E. Fraser, Ph.D.,
Lecturer in Early Scottish History and Culture,
University of Edinburgh

Reading Adviser: Alexa L. Sandmann, Ed.D., Professor of Literacy,
College and Graduate School of Education, Health,
and Human Services, Kent State University

COMPASS POINT BOOKS
a capstone imprint

Compass Point Books
151 Good Counsel Drive
P.O. Box 669
Mankato, MN 56002-0669

Editor: Brenda Haugen
Designer: Bobbie Nuytten
Media Researcher: Svetlana Zhurkin
Library Consultant: Kathleen Baxter
Production Specialist: Jane Klenk
Cartographer: XNR Productions, Inc.

Library of Congress Cataloging-in-Publication Data
Nardo, Don, 1947–
  Freedom fighter: William Wallace and Scotland's battle for
independence / by Don Nardo.
      p. cm.—(Taking a stand)
  Includes bibliographical references and index.
  ISBN 978-0-7565-4300-6 (library binding)
  1. Wallace, William, Sir, d. 1305—Juvenile literature. 2. Scotland—
History—Wallace's Rising, 1297–1304—Juvenile literature. 3. Revolutionaries—
Scotland—Biography—Juvenile literature. 4. Nationalists—Scotland—Biography—
Juvenile literature. 5. Guerrillas—Scotland—Biography—Juvenile literature. I. Title.
  DA783.3.N37 2010
  941.102—dc22   2009030369

Visit Compass Point Books on the Internet at www.compasspointbooks.com
or e-mail your request to custserv@compasspointbooks.com

IMAGE CREDITS

Alamy: Jason Friend 5, 56 (left), Scott MacQuarrie 20, Worldwide Picture Library 34; The Bridge-
man Art Library: Private Collection 23, 35, Private Collection/Look and Learn cover (top), 1, 28,
Private Collection/Peter Newark Pictures 33, Smith Art Gallery and Museum, Stirling, Scotland
45, 57 (left); Getty Images: Hulton Archive 9, 17, 43, 52, 54, 57 (right), Time & Life Pictures/
Mansell 13; iStockphoto: BMPix 55, Mark Hilverda cover (bottom); Mary Evans Picture Library
12, 14, 21, 41, 50; Shutterstock: Creative Hearts 26, 56 (right), Peter Guess 38.

TABLE OF CONTENTS

PROLOGUE

When I was growing up, I learned from a priest [a proverb that] I have carried [always] in my heart: 'I tell you the truth. Freedom is the finest of things. Never live [in bondage to others], my son.'

William Wallace's answer to the suggestion that the Scots submit to the English king

For seven centuries the people of Scotland have cherished and celebrated the memory of William Wallace. While some others view Wallace as an outlaw, in the eyes of the Scottish he is a national hero. In parts of the 13th and 14th centuries, Scotland was occupied by England. The Scots fought a series of battles to gain independence. Wallace emerged as one of the great freedom fighters of that age.

A statue of William Wallace stands near the Scottish village of Dryburgh.

Nothing certain is known about Wallace's youth. The medieval histories in which he appears say nothing about his early years. They first mention him when he was an adult and already fighting the English. Even the exact date and place of his birth are unclear and disputed. The best guess of modern scholars is that he was born in either 1272 or 1273.

During Wallace's childhood and early manhood, Scotland underwent a series of dramatic and turbulent events. These events are fairly well documented. So even though his personal life in these years is a mystery, we do have a good idea of what he witnessed. These events may largely explain why he decided to devote himself to the cause of Scottish freedom.

Still it is important to point out that extremely little reliable information about Wallace survived him. So writers in the generations that followed added "facts" of their own. This created a bigger, more exciting story than the short, uncertain one supported by the scant evidence. As a result, the William Wallace in modern books and films is to a large extent a legendary one. The aim of this book is to tell that legend while trying to separate facts from fiction wherever possible.

A MOST SPIRITED FIGHTING-MAN

A few descriptions of William Wallace's physical appearance and personality have survived. This one is from the *Scotichronicon*, a medieval Scottish chronicle. Because it was written well after his death, it may contain some exaggerations.

He was a tall man with the body of a giant, cheerful in appearance with agreeable features. [He was] broad-shouldered and big-boned, with belly in proportion [and] pleasing in appearance with a wild look, broad in the hips, with strong arms and legs. [He was] a most spirited fighting-man. [He also possessed] a certain good humor [and spoke so well that] he won over to himself the grace and favor of the hearts of all loyal Scots. And this is not surprising, for he was most liberal in all his gifts, very fair in his judgments, most compassionate in comforting the sad, a most skilled [adviser], very patient when suffering, [and] a distinguished speaker. [Above all, he] hunted down falsehood and deceit and detested treachery. [In addition, he] helped the poor and widows [and orphans], bringing relief to the oppressed. ... Because God was very greatly pleased with works of justice of this kind, He in consequence guided all [of Wallace's] activities.

CHAPTER ONE

A KING'S TRAGIC DEATH

Scotland was lost when he was but a child.

Blind Harry, a medieval Scottish poet, regretting that Scotland fell under the control of the English when Wallace was very young

At the time of William Wallace's birth, Scotland was ruled by King Alexander III. A capable and popular leader, Alexander maintained a friendly relationship with England. One way he cemented the peace was to marry Margaret, a daughter of England's King Henry III. Sadly for Alexander, she died in 1275, when Wallace was about 3 years old.

Scotland remained peaceful and prosperous until 1286, when sudden tragedy struck. On the night of March 19, King Alexander, then 44, and some companions dined in Edinburgh Castle in east-central Scotland. After eating they decided to travel to Fife, a region 22 miles (35 kilometers) to the north. The men mounted their horses and followed a trail along high bluffs on the north side of the Firth of Forth, the mouth of the River Forth, which is like an ocean bay.

It was a dark night, and sheets of rain were blowing in from the sea. This dangerous situation proved fatal for the king. He became

95 ALEXANDER III

Alexander III married Margaret, the daughter of Henry III, king of England. Henry often interfered in Scottish affairs.

separated from the others. His horse stumbled and sent him tumbling downhill, his body smashing against the jagged rocks as he went. In the morning, searchers found him on a beach beside the firth's waters. His neck was broken.

The heartbroken Scots grieved for their lost monarch. Wal-

lace, now about 14, and his family were almost surely among the

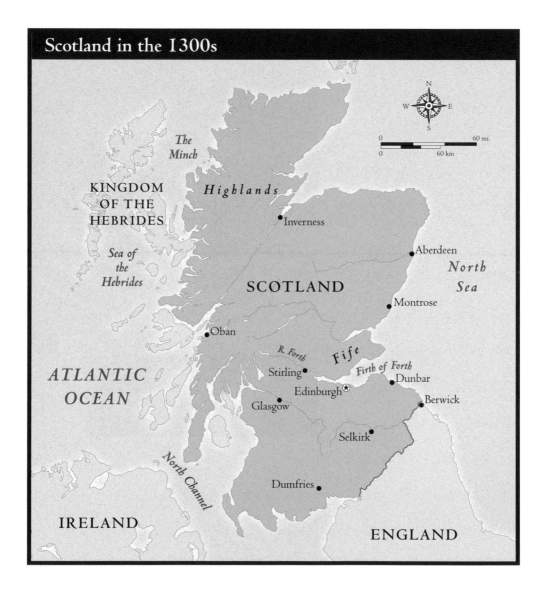

Scotland in the 1300s

The Minch

KINGDOM OF THE HEBRIDES

Highlands

Inverness

Aberdeen

North Sea

Sea of the Hebrides

SCOTLAND

Montrose

Oban

R. Forth

Fife

ATLANTIC OCEAN

Stirling

Firth of Forth

Dunbar

Edinburgh ✪

Berwick

Glasgow

Selkirk

North Channel

Dumfries

IRELAND

ENGLAND

mourners. Mixed with the sorrow were feelings of deep concern for the kingdom. Alexander had left no heir who could immediately take charge. His only living relative was a 3-year-old granddaughter named Margaret.

Scotland's leading nobles met in hope of resolving the crisis. They appointed six guardians to govern the country until Margaret was old enough to rule. A Scottish guardian was a powerful leader respected by the people. The six included two bishops and four wealthy noblemen.

Edward's Bold Power Play

At first the new arrangement seemed successful, but it did not last long. Margaret, who was sickly, died unexpectedly in September 1290, at age 7. The identity of the country's next ruler was once more in question. Several prominent nobles came forward and pressed their claims for the throne. Wallace was not among them because he was not of noble birth.

With so many men vying for power, the possibility of civil war soon loomed. To avoid such a conflict, the claimants called on an outsider to choose from among them. He was England's king, Edward I, nicknamed Longshanks. People also came to call him "the Hammer of the Scots" because he ended up opposing and trying to smash them for many years.

A strong, shrewd leader, Edward saw an opportunity to expand his power and influence. He agreed to pick a new Scottish monarch on the condition that the new Scottish king would owe him allegiance. Edward would be the real power behind Scotland's throne.

Edward was recognized as the overlord of Scotland, and claimants to the Scottish throne agreed to abide by his wishes.

The Scottish nobles did not like the deal they were offered, but they accepted it because they felt they had no other choice.

Edward's bold power play at first paid off for him. In November 1292, he chose one of the two leading claimants for the throne.

John Balliol was a well-meaning but weak leader. Edward liked the fact that he was weak, and he promptly crowned Balliol, who took the title King John.

Scotland's new leader had little to celebrate, however, because he had to do Edward's bidding. Most Scots, surely including William Wallace, found this humiliating. Edward also demanded that the Scots provide him with military aid in a war he planned against France. These moves aroused increasing anger among

John Balliol served as Scotland's king from 1292 until he gave up the throne in 1296.

the Scots. Matters came to a head in 1296. King John renounced his allegiance to the English king, and the two kingdoms prepared for war against one another.

No Option but Surrender

Ready to fight for their country, many Scots assembled at Caddonlee, in southern Scotland. Wallace, then about 24, was likely among them. These soldiers crossed into northern England and raided villages and farms. In retaliation, Edward gathered his troops and besieged the Scottish port town of Berwick. Unable to resist the barrage of English battering rams, arrows, and catapulted rocks, Berwick

Edward took the strategic town of Berwick, near the border of England and Scotland, and claimed it for England.

quickly fell. According to a medieval chronicler: "Sparing neither sex nor age, [Edward] put to the sword 7,500 [Scots], so that, for two days streams [of blood] flowed from the bodies of the slain." Soon afterward one of Edward's chief nobles defeated a small Scottish army at Dunbar, on the coast east of Edinburgh.

His forces defeated and scattered, King John saw no option but surrender. In July 1296, he handed over his kingdom to the English. The triumphant Edward sent the disgraced Scottish king to England's most infamous prison, the Tower of London. There John found himself alone in a dreary cell, cut off from most news about his countrymen.

Edward tightened his grip on Scotland. In August he summoned the leading Scottish nobles and churchmen to Berwick. In a triumphant tone, he forced them to swear allegiance to him. He then returned to England, confident that Scotland would cause him no more trouble. He was wrong. He had no way of knowing that an obscure Scot named William Wallace would soon rally the Scots in a daring bid for freedom.

CHAPTER TWO

FROM OUTLAW TO FREEDOM FIGHTER

There flocked to him all who were in bitterness of spirit, and weighed down beneath the burden of bondage under the unbearable domination of English despotism, and he became their leader.

A medieval Scottish chronicler on William Wallace's rise to power

It was no secret that King Edward had no love or respect for the Scots, and he was glad to put the conquest of Scotland behind him. It is said that as he was crossing the border into England he remarked, "He who rids himself of [bodily waste] does a good job."

But Edward was far from rid of the Scots. They deeply resented Edward's recent suppression of them. As soon as he left, some Scots began to plot a rebellion. The first leaders of the uprising were high-born men. They included an influential bishop named Robert Wishart and popular noblemen James the Stewart and Robert Bruce.

The men soon viewed their high social standing as an obstacle, however. They had just pledged their loyalty to Edward and promised to keep the peace. That put them in an awkward and dangerous position. If the rebellion failed, they and their families and followers would lose everything. This may have been why they turned to William Wallace

Robert Bruce was a fierce warrior and eventually became Scotland's king.

for help. They found that he was more than willing to risk his life for the cause of Scottish freedom.

The Rogue of Selkirk Forest

There was likely another reason that Wallace swiftly rose to an important position in the resistance. He had gained a reputation as a formidable fighting man. How he acquired his military skills is unknown. Perhaps seeking money or adventure, he might have hired himself out as a soldier. Several small wars and rebellions occurred in Britain and western Europe in the late 1280s and early 1290s. Wallace may have taken part in one or more of them.

Wallace's military skills also may have come from his exploits as the leader of a band of outlaws. Several medieval chronicles suggest that in the early 1290s, Wallace was sort of like Robin Hood. The English Robin was famous for dashing through the forest to help the poor, slaying evil tax collectors with his trusty bow, and defeating the enemies of the rightful king. Such stories may be little more than folklore. The same may be true about the tales that picture Wallace as a heroic outlaw. However, some historians suspect that they contain at least some truth.

The most famous version of how Wallace became an outlaw is likely fictional, but it may have been based on a similar event that was not recorded. It begins with his living in Irvine, in southwestern Scotland. He was fishing in a river when five English soldiers rode up and demanded he give them the fish he'd caught. Wallace offered them half, but they repeated their demand for the entire catch.

Wallace wasn't the type of person who could be bullied, so a fight began. He drew his sword, and when a soldier lunged at him, he disarmed the man. But the others were soon upon him. In a brilliant display of fighting ability, Wallace killed three of the attackers. The other two escaped and reported the incident to the English authorities. Worried that he would be arrested, Wallace's relatives urged him to flee. He headed eastward into Selkirk Forest. There many men flocked to him and helped him raid English lands.

Wallace Raises His Head

The better documented episodes of Wallace's life began early in 1297, shortly after King Edward returned to England. In one

William Wallace's sword is on display at a monument named for him in Stirling, Scotland.

medieval chronicler's words, Wallace "raised his head." This meant that he suddenly rose from the realm of hearsay into the provable pages of history.

The first event that pushed Wallace into the public eye involved a woman's death. Medieval accounts claimed she was his wife and that her name was Marion Braidfute. Some modern scholars think she might have been legendary, or at least that her role in Wallace's story might have been exaggerated. In any case, according to the medieval accounts, Wallace's and Braidfute's marriage was known to only a few. But one of King Edward's followers, William Heselrig, found out. Heselrig, the sheriff of Lanark, which was north of Selkirk Forest, decided to hurt Wallace by killing his wife. Heselrig stabbed Braidfute to death. As her blood stained the floors of her home, Heselrig burned it down.

The news of Braidfute's death soon reached Wallace. Filled with grief and rage, he screamed in agony and vowed to get revenge. He and some companions wasted no time in raiding Lanark and slaying the sheriff in a gruesome manner. According to the later medieval Scottish poet Blind Harry, whose account likely contains fictional elements: "Gathering together a band of desperate men, [Wallace] fell by night on the sheriff and his armed guard, hewed [sliced] the sheriff into small pieces with his own sword and burned [Heselrig's] buildings and those within them."

Joining Forces

Heselrig's dramatic slaying made his killer a high-profile leader in the Scottish resistance. Many

Wallace killed a soldier in Lanark before making his escape to safety.

patriotic Scots joined Wallace. As a medieval writer told it: "He manfully [devoted] himself to the storming of the castles and fortified towns in which the English ruled. For he aimed at quickly and thoroughly freeing his country and overthrowing the enemy."

Wallace's first target was Scone, in central Scotland just north of Fife. An important leader of the English occupation, William Ormsby, was stationed there. Ormsby managed to escape, but Wallace's success at Scone frightened other Englishmen in the region.

Hearing of the renewed rebellion in Scotland, Edward was enraged. He sent a force of soldiers to arrest the leaders of the uprising. Once more the Scottish nobles backed down. Several of them surrendered without a fight and were carted away to English prisons.

Wallace may have been disgusted by what he probably saw as a cowardly display by his countrymen. He continued to attack English strongholds. In August 1297, he laid siege to one of the most formidable of these—the castle at Dundee, a few miles east of Scone. Arrows and rocks from Wallace's men rained down on the fortress, whose soldiers finally surrendered.

King Edward sent his forces north to Scotland.

As Wallace swept through south-ern Scotland, he kept in touch with Andrew Moray, a fellow freedom fighter in the north. Moray had been captured by the English in the battle at Dunbar the year before. A few months later, he had escaped and made his way back to his home in northern Scotland. There he had gathered followers and begun attacking English-occupied towns and castles.

Wallace and Moray joined forces at Dundee in September 1297. By this time, news had come that a large English army was heading northward toward Stirling, in central Scotland. Wallace and Moray were determined to stop the invaders. Gathering their combined forces, they hurried westward toward Stirling.

HERO OF THE HIGHLAND REBELLION

This overview of Andrew Moray's exploits was written by Donald Urquhart, a descendant of one of the Scottish families whose lands were occupied by the English in the late 1200s:

After his escape and travels across wintry England and Scotland, Andrew Moray finally managed to make it back to [Moray, in northern Scotland]. He unfurled the banner of the Morays [over] his castle at Avoch in defiance of Edward in May of 1297. ... This was the same month that William Wallace kicked off his Lowlands rebellion. News of Andrew's escape, return, and defiance quickly drew followers like moths to a flame. ... English [officials] in the [region] were cut off from English support by Andrew's actions. [Englishman] William fitz Warin, keeper of Castle Urquhart, was on his way home from an English officials' meeting at the castle of Inverness when Andrew ambushed him. [William] was besieged by Andrew, who attempted to gain control of the castle directly several times, including a night attack. Andrew [did] eventually take Castle Urquhart, along with all the other [English-held] fortifications [in the area]. Andrew's campaigns continued unabated due to the massive support he enjoyed from the Highlands. Throughout the summer of 1297, he continued to make the English in northern Scotland miserable. His brilliant military campaign bore fruit as English-held castles fell to him one after the other.

CHAPTER THREE

THE BATTLE OF STIRLING BRIDGE

Tell your people that we have not come here to gain peace, but are prepared for battle, to avenge and [free] our country. ... They will find us ready to meet them even to their beards!

William Wallace's answer to the English demand for his surrender in the hours before the Battle of Stirling Bridge

The English were headed for Stirling because of its strategic location. It was in Scotland's narrow middle region, which divides the country's southern and northern sections. Heavily fortified Stirling Castle loomed on a high bluff overlooking the town. Anyone who commanded the castle and surrounding area controlled the main route into northern Scotland. Capturing Stirling would give the

Stirling Castle sits high atop a volcanic outcrop.

English a major advantage. The Scots would also benefit greatly from a victory at Stirling. It would confine the English to southern Scotland, making their conquest of the kingdom harder.

The Opposing Armies

The Scots arrived at Stirling before the English did. Wallace and Moray positioned their forces on a wooded hillside north of the Forth River. This waterway flows into the Firth of Forth. On its way, it moves through an expanse of flat meadows to the east of Stirling Castle. The only way for the English to cross the river was over Stirling Bridge, a large wooden structure. Wallace's and Moray's plan was to halt the invaders' northward advance in whatever way they could.

The Scots had about 7,000 men. Most were infantrymen, 6,000 spearmen and about 400 archers. The cavalrymen, who were soldiers on horses, numbered about 180. (It's hard to know whether these and other figures for medieval armies are accurate. The real numbers might have been exaggerated in repeated retellings over the years.)

The Scots relied heavily on their infantry, especially the spearmen. A more accurate term for them would be pikemen. Their spears were unusually long—from 12 to 14 feet (3.7 to 4.3 meters). Spears that long are also called pikes. In those days, Scottish infantrymen usually fought in battlefield formations called schiltrons. Each consisted of a large group of pikemen standing close together in lines one behind another. The pikemen often formed a big circle. But schiltrons were sometimes rectangular, as they were at Stirling. Using two hands, each man in a schiltron pointed his pike toward the enemy. That created a thick wall of pike points that could mow down ordinary spearmen or swordsmen.

On September 11, 1297, the English arrived at Stirling and approached the bridge. From their vantage point on the hill, the Scots could see that the armies were roughly equal in size. The

English force had about 6,300 infantrymen, archers, swordsmen, and ordinary spearmen. There were also about 350 knights and other horsemen.

Serious Errors in Judgment

Neither side enjoyed a numerical advantage. However, the Scots had another kind of advantage—the incompetence and overconfidence of the English commanders. King Edward had entrusted the campaign to John de Warenne, the Earl of Surrey, an experienced but third-rate military

William Wallace and his Scottish freedom fighters battled ferociously.

leader. Aiding Warenne was Hugh de Cressingham, Edward's trea-

surer in Scotland. Cressingham was a grossly overweight, arrogant,

and talentless man. Most Englishmen hated him nearly as much as

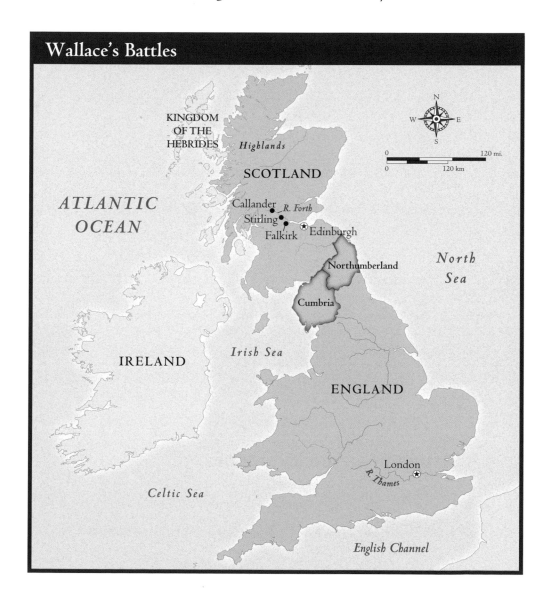

Wallace's Battles

the Scots did. Both Warenne and Cressingham viewed the Scots as disorganized, ineffective fighters. They believed Wallace and Moray had no chance against English gentlemen like themselves.

In addition to these errors in judgment, the English commanders made a serious tactical mistake. In preparation for battle, Wallace and Moray had already formed their schiltrons about two-thirds of a mile (1 km) north of the bridge. The English could see the schiltrons, with their murderous mass of pike points extending outward. Once given the order to attack, the Scots could easily reach the bridge in about 10 minutes.

Ignoring this dangerous possibility, Warenne and Cressingham told their troops to begin crossing the bridge. But the bridge was so narrow that only a few men could fit on it at one time. So moving the entire English army across the river would require hours.

Slaughter on the Riverbank

The English blunder must have been immediately apparent to Wallace and Moray. They waited patiently until about 2,000 of the enemy had crossed the bridge. Then Wallace ordered the Scots to

THE ENGLISH CROSS THE BRIDGE

In his account of the battle, medieval chronicler Walter of Guisborough described what happened when the English commanders unwisely ordered their men to cross the narrow bridge:

> *[The Earl of Surrey] commanded that [the men in the front ranks] should go up to the bridge and cross it. It was astonishing to say, and terrible in its consequence, that such a large number of individual men, though they knew the enemy was at hand, should go up to a narrow bridge which a pair of horsemen could scarcely and with difficulty cross at the same time. Since, as some who had been in the same conflict were saying, if they had crossed over from earliest morning until the eleventh hour, without any interruption or hindrance, the last part of the army would have remained [behind] in great part until then. Nor was there a more appropriate place in the kingdom of Scotland for shutting the English into the hands of the Scots, and the many into the hands of the few. So there crossed over the King's and the Earl's standard-bearers [followed by many soldiers].*

attack. Like giant hedgehogs with their spines erect, the schiltrons, bristling with pike points, surged forward.

Seeing these frightening formations approaching, the English soldiers were gripped with fear. Backing up, they gathered in disorganized masses on the river's north bank. Some desperately tried to organize into a battle formation. Others panicked and tried to retreat over the bridge, but its narrowness allowed only a handful to escape.

A few minutes later, the Scottish schiltrons arrived with a fury. They smashed into the chaotic English ranks. Many English soldiers were driven back into the river, where they drowned. Most of the rest of their comrades were slaughtered on the riverbank. Several Scots dragged Cressingham from his horse, pulled out knives, and butchered him like an animal. According to a medieval writer: "He who had previously terrified many by the sword of his tongue in many court trials, was eventually slain by the sword. ... The Scots stripped him of his skin and divided it amongst themselves in small parts." Wallace was said to have made a belt from it.

Meanwhile the main body of the English army, under Warenne,

As the Stirling Bridge collapsed, the battle raged on.

still stood on the south side of the river. The men watched the hideous massacre in horror. Warenne seems to have feared that the victorious Scots would next cross the bridge and attack him. He ordered his men to demolish the south end of the bridge. Then he mounted his horse. His face drawn into a mask of fear, he fled, abandoning his troops.

An Adept Ruler

The consequences of the Scottish victory at Stirling Bridge were far-reaching. William Wallace became a national hero and the undisputed leader of Scotland. Andrew Moray, who was mortally wounded in the battle, died less than two months later.

The triumph at Stirling also roused the Scots to expand the war effort. In the months that followed, they drove nearly all the English occupiers out of the country.

The Scots now had a leader with talent and popularity unmatched since the death of Alexander III. They soon expressed their gratitude. On March 29, 1298, they appointed Wallace sole guardian of Scotland.

This confidence in Wallace was not misplaced. He soon

A plaque at the site of the Stirling Bridge battle pays tribute to those who fought there for freedom.

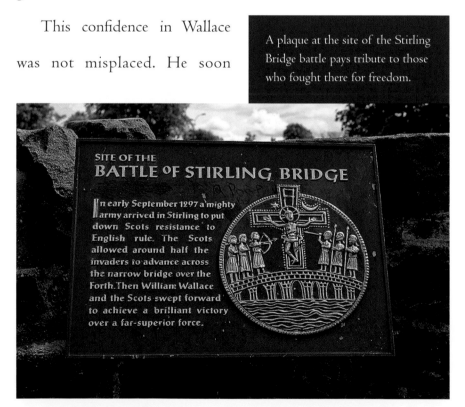

SITE OF THE
BATTLE OF STIRLING BRIDGE

In early September 1297 a mighty army arrived in Stirling to put down Scots resistance to English rule. The Scots allowed around half the invaders to advance across the narrow bridge over the Forth. Then William Wallace and the Scots swept forward to achieve a brilliant victory over a far-superior force.

proved himself as adept at ruling as he was at fighting. Only weeks after the battle at Stirling, he began to rebuild Scotland's foreign trade. Under Alexander, the nation had grown prosperous from trade with European kingdoms and cities. The fighting in Scotland had caused commerce to seriously decline. Wallace sent letters to European leaders telling them that Scotland was once again open for business.

In spite of his leadership skills, Wallace could not predict how Edward would react to the loss of Scotland. The English king was furious. He immediately began preparing a new and bigger invasion force. Once more Wallace would be called on to save his country.

WALLACE'S LETTER TO THE GERMANS

One of Wallace's letters on trade, written while Moray was still hanging onto life, has survived. It was addressed to the Hanseatic League, an alliance of northern German trading cities. Wallace wrote:

Andrew Moray and William Wallace, leaders of the Scotch army, and the commonwealth of the same kingdom send to the prudent and discreet men, our good friends, the Senate and the commoners of Lubeck and of Hamburg [two leading cities in the league] greeting and a continuous increase of sincere affection. We have been informed by trustworthy merchants of the said kingdom of Scotland, that you on your own behalf have been friendly and helpful in counsel and deed in all things and enterprises concerning us and our merchants. ... We are therefore the more beholden to you, and wishing to prove our gratitude in a worthy manner we ask you to make it known among your merchants that they can now have a safe access with their merchandise to all harbors of the Kingdom of Scotland, because the Kingdom of Scotland has, thanks be to God, by war been recovered from the power of the English. Farewell. Given at Haddington in Scotland on the eleventh day of October in the year of Grace one thousand two hundred and ninety seven.

CHAPTER FOUR

SCOTLAND'S GUARDIAN STEPS DOWN

I have brought you to the revel [party]. Now dance if you can!

William Wallace to his soldiers in the minutes before the Battle of Falkirk

The winter of 1297–1298 was a busy time for William Wallace. Not only did he become guardian of Scotland, he also was knighted. The identity of the person who knighted him is unknown. Medieval sources say only that it was a high-born Scottish earl. At that time, any member of the nobility could make someone a knight.

Assault on Northern England

Wallace also took the fight for Scottish independence directly to the English. That winter he gathered about 100 horsemen and about 3,000 foot soldiers. With them he crossed the border into northern England and pillaged the counties of Northumberland and Cumbria. Smoke poured into the sky and bodies littered the fields as many houses, farms, and villages throughout these regions were destroyed.

Wallace especially wanted to capture Carlisle Castle in Cumbria. This stronghold was an important supply base for English invasions of Scotland. According to the medieval chronicler Walter of Guisborough, Wallace sent the castle's commander the following message: "[I] command you to have care for your lives and to yield this town and castle

Carlisle Castle, near the border of England and Scotland, is more than 900 years old.

WALLACE RAIDS ENGLAND

This account of Wallace's attacks on northern England is from a medieval document called the *Lanercost Chronicle*. Partly because it was written by an Englishman who had suffered at the hands of the Scots, it portrays Wallace and his men as savage murderers:

> *After these events [the Scottish victory at Stirling Bridge and Warenne's flight back into England], the Scots [under the command of Wallace] entered Northumberland in strength. [They wasted] all the land, committing arson, pillage, and murder, and advancing almost as far as the town of Newcastle. From [there], however, they turned aside and entered the county of Carlisle. There they did as they had done in Northumberland, destroying everything, then returned into Northumberland to lay waste more completely what they had left at first, and reentered Scotland on the Feast of St. Cecelia [November 22].*

... without bloodshed. [If you do, I] will grant you your lives and limbs and all your beasts. If you will not do this, [I] will immediately attack you and destroy you utterly."

The commander refused to surrender, so the Scots prepared for a siege. It never took place, however. Wanting to avoid getting bogged down too long in Cumbria, Wallace decided to lead most of his forces southward into Durham County. Fortunately for the English, a heavy snowstorm stopped the invaders. Caught in below-freezing temperatures and blinded by the howling blizzard, Wallace and his men returned to Scotland.

The Battle of Falkirk

During the same months, King Edward and other English leaders were not idle. All across England many soldiers were being recruited. The king was determined to punish the Scots for their victory at Stirling Bridge and to regain control of Scotland. Having raised an army, Edward began his northward march in May 1298. He entered southern Scotland in July.

Wallace was aware of the English advance. He, too, had been

Wallace inspired his men
as he led them into battle.

raising troops. He correctly reasoned that Edward

would first try to recapture Stirling Castle. That

would give the English a strong base from which to attack both

southern and northern Scotland. So Wallace positioned his army to

the south of Stirling, near the town of Falkirk. At first Edward had

no idea where the opposing army was. Then one of his spies told

him where Wallace's forces were camped. The English army arrived

at Falkirk just before dawn on July 22, 1298.

Later that morning, Edward and his officers could see the

Scots. The best guess of scholars is that they were in a meadow

about 1 mile (1.6 km) away, in front of a forest called Callendar

Wood. It was clear that this time the English had the numerical advantage. Edward had about 2,250 cavalrymen and nearly 13,000 infantrymen. Wallace had barely 500 cavalrymen and only 9,500 infantrymen. The Scots formed four large circular schiltrons. Between these Wallace placed most of his archers. Riding back and forth on his horse, he delivered a rousing battle speech that echoed across the fields.

Minutes later Edward's cavalrymen attacked. Thundering across the meadows, they created a startling and scary image. Fearing certain death, most of the Scottish horsemen, including Wallace, retreated from the field. Then the English horsemen charged toward the waiting schiltrons. The Scottish infantrymen dug in their heels and bravely held their ground. Their attackers could make no dent in the sturdy walls of outward-pointing pikes. For a while, the fight remained a stalemate, while a deafening din of pounding hooves and soldiers' shouts filled the air.

Then Edward brought up his archers, who numbered almost 6,000. Some wielded English longbows, which fired traditional arrows. Others carried crossbows, which unleashed large, lethal darts called bolts. In volley after volley, the arrows and bolts poured into the Scottish infantrymen. This caused mass deaths in the schiltrons' ranks, which heaved back and forth under the relentless rain of missiles. As the great circles shrank and fell apart, some of the Scots ran for the nearby forest. The English horsemen pursued and mercilessly killed many of them.

The battle at Falkirk was a blow to the Scottish freedom fighters.

A Damaged Reputation

The number of casualties suffered by both sides at Falkirk remains uncertain. There is little doubt, though, that thousands of Scots died in the battle. Edward had won a stunning victory.

Yet the king realized that Scotland was far from beaten. He managed to recapture Stirling Castle. His forces raided and burned many towns in southern Scotland. But most of the northern highlands remained beyond his grasp. In a letter sent in August 1298 to Edward's treasurer, an English officer at Edinburgh Castle wrote: "[A number of rebellious Scottish] earls and lords, who were on the [northern] side of the [Firth of Forth] have come to this side. Today they are in Glasgow. They intend to [raid] towards the border, as is reported among them and their people who are in the forest."

Although the Scottish resistance was still intact, Wallace's reputation was not. Many Scots still respected him. They admired his continued devotion to the cause of freedom. But the horrific losses at Falkirk had dealt that cause a devastating blow. Most felt that they could no longer trust Wallace with its leadership. Wallace seems to have understood this reality. He did the honorable thing and stepped down from the office of guardian. As a later medieval writer said: "[Wallace] chose rather to serve with the crowd [put himself at the people's level] than to be [a ruler] over them, to their ruin, and the grievous [harm] of the people. So, not long after the battle of Falkirk, at the water of Forth, he, of his own accord, resigned the office and charge which he held, of Guardian."

Wallace Goes to Europe

Even before he resigned, Wallace did not pretend to be Scotland's king. He still strongly supported John Balliol's title to that office. King John had abdicated the throne in 1296.

A 19th century oil painting at the Smith Art Gallery and Museum in Stirling shows how William Wallace might have looked.

After being released from the Tower of London, he had been allowed to settle in France. But Wallace and many other Scots remained true to him. They clung to the notion that he would someday return and reclaim the throne.

Hoping to help make that happen, in 1299 Wallace went to Europe. He visited France, Norway, Italy, and perhaps other countries where Scottish ambassadors had been arguing for their cause for some time. In each place, he met with local leaders. On behalf of John, he asked them to help Scotland gain independence.

None of the European rulers Wallace met with offered him much aid. They did not want to risk angering King Edward. So Wallace returned to Scotland. There he hoped to continue the fight against the English. He hoped he would live to see the day that Scotland was fully free. But that was not to be.

A LETTER FROM KING PHILIP

Part of the evidence for Wallace's trip to Europe is a letter written by the French king, Philip IV. In it Philip asks his ambassadors to the Vatican, in Rome, to welcome Wallace when he arrives in that city to meet with the pope:

Philip, by the grace of God, King of the French, [writes this] to my loved and faithful, my [ambassadors], appointed to the Roman court, greetings and love. We command you to request the supreme Pontiff to hold our beloved William the Waleis, of Scotland, [a] knight, recommended to his [the pope's] favor, in those things which with him he has to dispatch [the business Wallace and the pope will discuss]. Given at Pierrefonds [in France], on Monday after the feast of All Saints [November 1].

CHAPTER FIVE

WALLACE'S CAPTURE AND LAST DAYS

Even if all Scots obey the king of England, so that each one abandons his liberty, I and my companions ... shall stand up for the liberty of the [Scottish] kingdom. And may God be favorable to us.

William Wallace's refusal to surrender to the English king after other Scottish leaders had done so

King Edward returned to England in the fall of 1298 a dissatis-fied man. He had soundly defeated the Scots at Falkirk. Then his soldiers had laid waste to large sections of southern Scotland. Yet Scottish resistance to his authority continued. After William Wal-lace had resigned as guardian, the Scottish nobles replaced him with John Comyn and Robert Bruce. In the years that followed, a series of other men took on the job of guardian. In fact there seemed to be no shortage of Scots who were willing to oppose the English occupation.

An Unending Nuisance

Edward was just as stubborn as his Scottish adversaries. Intent on conquering them, he launched new invasions of Scotland. In the summer of 1300, he managed to capture a few Scottish castles. He also defeated the Scots in a small battle at the Cree River in southwest Scotland. Yet these events had little impact on the ongoing war between the two countries. Scotland remained rebellious and a seemingly unending nuisance to Edward. Hoping to rid himself of the problem, he entered Scotland again the following year. But this operation was even less successful than the preceding one.

Edward achieved a great deal more when he invaded Scotland yet again in 1303–1304. His forces overran large parts of the country. Even much of the northern highlands region came under his control. Edward was so successful that most of the main Scottish leaders surrendered.

Wallace was not among them. He refused to give up the fight.

Wallace faced Edward's forces in many battles, and Edward desperately wanted to capture or kill him.

For a while, he was the only major Scottish figure who kept the rebellion alive. In part this was because Edward had promised to give clemency to other Scottish leaders who surrendered, but he had refused to offer clemency to Wallace.

Wallace's Capture

Edward hated Wallace and set his sights on capturing and making an example of him. To this end, Edward threatened to banish John Comyn and several other Scottish lords if they did not help to hunt Wallace down. The king said he would "show more favor to the man that shall have captured Wallace." This favor would consist of "shortening his term of exile, diminishing the amount of his ransom ... or otherwise lightening his liabilities [burdens]."

Comyn and other Scottish leaders refused to go after Wallace, and he remained at large. Most of the time he was in hiding. Some evidence suggests that from time to time he emerged to conduct raids against the English occupiers.

But not all of the high-placed Scots who knew Wallace were willing to protect him. On August 3, 1305, John Menteith, a knight and the son of a Scottish lord, made sure Wallace would be captured. At midnight Menteith led a small force of English soldiers to the place where Wallace was sleeping. A fight began. Using his bare hands, Wallace broke a soldier's back and smashed another's skull, sending the men sprawling to the floor. More attackers came at him, and he resisted with every ounce of strength, but the odds against him were too great. Still thrashing and struggling, he was dragged away in chains.

Wallace's Execution

The soldiers took Wallace to London. There Edward enjoyed the public spectacle of his enemy's condemnation and execution. On August 23, the English government produced a list of charges against Wallace. The charges included a wide range of crimes. Among them were killing the sheriff of Lanark in 1297, invading northern England, and fighting battles against King Edward.

The charges were no more than a formality. Only minutes after they were read aloud, the judges, picked by Edward, sentenced Wallace to death. The sentence was carried out the same day. In a disgusting display of cruelty, Wallace was hanged, disemboweled, decapitated, and cut into pieces.

His Memory Lives

William Wallace's final suffering, like his tireless efforts to free Scotland, was

Wallace was led through London to Westminster Hall, where he was found guilty of treason.

A FELON AND ENEMY OF PEACE

The indictment against Wallace has survived. In part it says that Wallace, by invading the northern English counties:

> *had feloniously [criminally] slain all he had found in those places [and] had not spared any person that spoke the English tongue. ... He had slain the priests and nuns, and burned down the churches [and] in such ways, day by day and hour by hour, he had [continued his crimes], to the danger alike of the life and crown of the Lord King [Edward]. For all that, when the Lord King invaded Scotland [and] defeated William, who opposed him in a pitched battle, [afterwards Edward] had mercifully [offered to make peace with Wallace]. Yet William, [continuing] in his wickedness, had rejected [Edward's peace offerings] with indignant scorn, and refused to submit himself to the King's peace. Therefore, in the court of the Lord King, [Wallace] had been publicly outlawed [as] a robber and a felon [criminal].*

not in vain. The Scots continued to resist the English occupation. In 1306, less than a year after Wallace's death, Robert Bruce proclaimed himself king of Scotland. In 1314 at Bannockburn near Falkirk, Bruce soundly defeated Edward's son and successor, Edward II. In 1328 King Edward III gave up all English claims to Scotland, making it a free nation.

In the centuries that followed, each new Scottish generation honored Wallace as one of the nation's great heroes and added new stories to the growing Wallace legend. In 1869 the Scots erected a monument

The defeat of the English at Bannockburn proved to be an important battle in the fight for Scottish freedom.

to him. With its spires soaring about 220 feet (67 meters) into the sky, it stands at Stirling, the site of his greatest victory. Wallace's courage and determination also inspired people around the world. He became the subject of countless poems and books, as well as the Oscar-winning 1995 film *Braveheart*.

A monument was erected in Stirling in honor of Wallace and his fight for Scottish freedom.

Wallace's memory also lives in Scotland's declaration of independence. Known as the Declaration of Arbroath, it was written 15 years after Wallace's death. Its most famous lines closely echo Wallace's feelings about human liberty: "As long as but a hundred of us remain alive, never will we on any conditions be brought under English rule. It is in truth not for glory, nor riches, nor honors that we are fighting, but for freedom—for that alone, which no honest man gives up but with life itself."

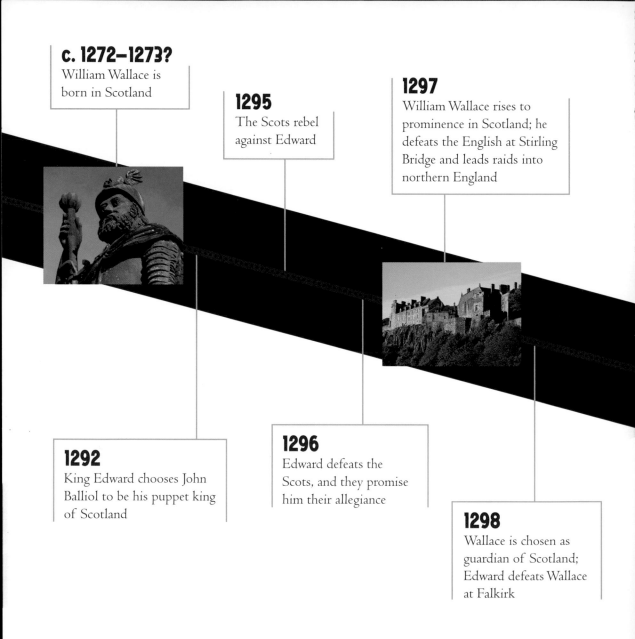

c. 1272–1273?
William Wallace is born in Scotland

1295
The Scots rebel against Edward

1297
William Wallace rises to prominence in Scotland; he defeats the English at Stirling Bridge and leads raids into northern England

1292
King Edward chooses John Balliol to be his puppet king of Scotland

1296
Edward defeats the Scots, and they promise him their allegiance

1298
Wallace is chosen as guardian of Scotland; Edward defeats Wallace at Falkirk

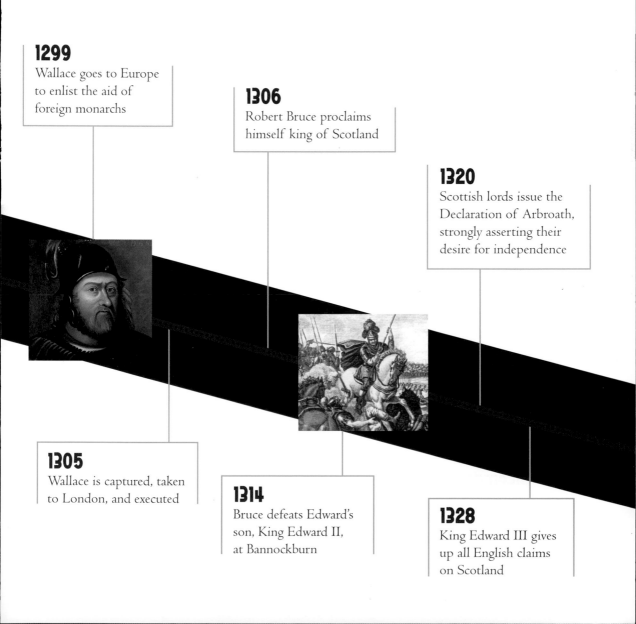

1299
Wallace goes to Europe
to enlist the aid of
foreign monarchs

1306
Robert Bruce proclaims
himself king of Scotland

1320
Scottish lords issue the
Declaration of Arbroath,
strongly asserting their
desire for independence

1305
Wallace is captured, taken
to London, and executed

1314
Bruce defeats Edward's
son, King Edward II,
at Bannockburn

1328
King Edward III gives
up all English claims
on Scotland

GLOSSARY

abdicate: voluntarily give up a royal throne

cavalrymen: soldiers who ride horses

clemency: mercy when deciding on a punishment

crossbow: mechanical bow used in medieval warfare

decapitated: form of execution in which one's head is cut off

despotism: tyranny or dictatorship

disembowelled: medieval punishment in which one's abdomen is sliced open and the intestines are removed

firth: ocean inlet or river

formidable: impressively strong

guardian: respected person chosen to lead the country in the absence of a king

incompetence: being inept or lacking skill

indictment: document charging a person with a crime

infantrymen: foot soldiers

laurel: wreath made from the leaves of an evergreen bush

pillaged: robbed by force, especially during war

renounced: gave up, abandoned, or resigned, usually by a public declaration

rogue: rascal or crook

schiltron: battlefield formation made of soldiers holding long spears, also called pikes

stalemate: situation in which neither of two opponents can defeat the other

suppression: put down by authority or force

tactical: having to do with an immediate goal, as in military maneuvers during battle

ADDITIONAL RESOURCES

Further Reading

Henty, George Alfred. *In Freedom's Cause.* Charlottesville, Va.:
Greathall Productions, 2006.

Ross, David R. *For Freedom: The Last Days of William Wallace.*
Edinburgh, Scotland: Luath Press, 2007.

Ross, David R. *The Story of Robert Bruce.* Santa Monica, Calif.:
Waverley Books, 2006.

Vanderwal, Andrew H. *The Battle for Duncragglin.* Toronto:
Tundra Books, 2009.

Woodruff, Elvira. *The Ravenmaster's Secret: Escape From the Tower
of London.* New York: Scholastic Press, 2003.

Yolen, Jane. *Prince Across the Water.* New York: Philomel
Books, 2004.

Internet Sites

FactHound offers a safe, fun way to find Internet sites related to this book. All of the sites on FactHound have been researched by our staff.

Here's all you do:
    Visit *www.facthound.com*
FactHound will fetch the best sites for you.

Look for more *Taking a Stand* books:

Refusing to Crumble: The Danish Resistance in World War II
Striking Back: The Fight to End Child Labor Exploitation
United in Cause: The Sons of Liberty

SELECT BIBLIOGRAPHY

Armstrong, Pete. *Stirling Bridge and Falkirk: William Wallace's Rebellion, 1297–98.* Westport, Conn.: Praeger, 2005.

Brown, Chris. *The Second Scottish Wars of Independence.* Stroud, Gloucestershire, England: Tempus, 2006.

Fisher, Andrew. *William Wallace.* Edinburgh, Scotland: Birlinn, 2007.

Mackay, James A. *William Wallace: Brave Heart.* Edinburgh, Scotland: Mainstream Publishing, 1996.

Mitchison, Rosalind. *A History of Scotland.* London: Routledge, 2002.

Morton, Graeme. *William Wallace: Man and Myth.* Stroud, Gloucestershire, England: Sutton Publishing, 2004.

Murison, Alexander Falconer. *William Wallace: Guardian of Scotland.* Mineola, N.Y.: Dover Publications, 2003.

Reese, Peter. *Wallace: A Biography.* Edinburgh, Scotland: Canongate, 1996.

Rothwell, Harry, ed. *The Chronicle of Walter of Guisborough.* London: Offices of the Royal Historical Society, 1957.

Young, Alan, and Michael J. Stead. *In the Footsteps of Robert Bruce.* Stroud, Gloucestershire, England: Sutton Publishing, 1999.

SOURCE NOTES

Chapter 1: James A. Mackay. *William Wallace: Brave Heart.* Edinburgh, Scotland: Mainstream Publishing, 1996, p. 67.

Chapter 2: Felix Skene. *John of Fordun's Chronicle of the Scottish Nation.* 27 Oct. 2009. www.archive.org/stream/johnoffordunschr00fordrich/johnoffordunschr-00fordrich_djvu.txt

Donald Urquhart. "Andrew Moray: An Unsung Warrior and Hero of Scotland and Her Highlands." 27 Oct. 2009. www.historyandlegends.com/andrew-moray-scotlands-highland-warrior.html

Chapter 3: *William Wallace: Brave Heart*, p. 146.

"Stirling Bridge, 1297: William Wallace and Andrew Moray Defeat the English." 27 Oct. 2009. www.nls.uk/scotlandspages/timeline/1297.html

"The Scots in Germany." 27 Oct. 2009. www.electricscotland.com/history/germany/commerce.htm

Chapter 4: Pete Armstrong. *Stirling Bridge and Falkirk: William Wallace's Rebellion, 1297–98.* Westport, Conn.: Praeger, 2005, p. 73.

Lanercost Chronicle. 27 Oct. 2009. http://openlibrary.org/details/chronicleoflaner00maxwuoft

William Wallace: Brave Heart, p. 163.

Chapter 5: N.F. Shead. *Scotichronicon by Walter Bower.* Aberdeen, Scotland: Aberdeen University Press, 1991, p. 299.

William Wallace: Brave Heart, pp. 189–190.

INDEX

ABOUT THE AUTHOR

In addition to his acclaimed volumes on the ancient world, historian and award-winning author Don Nardo has produced several studies of medieval times and books about medieval figures. Nardo lives with his wife, Christine, in Massachusetts.